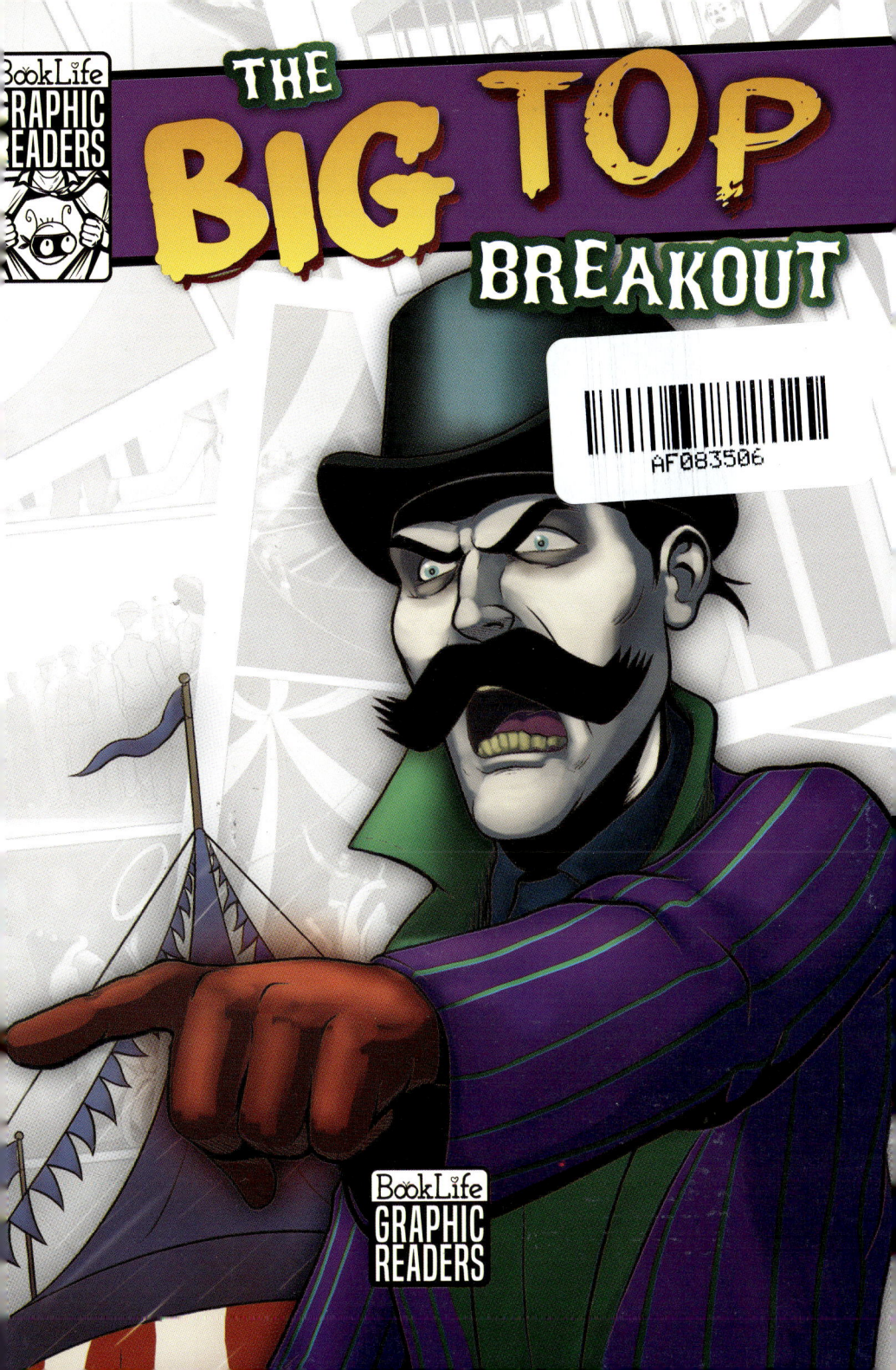

HOW TO READ A COMIC BOOK

Comic books are made up of pictures in boxes, called panels. Look at each of these panels from left to right, and top to bottom.

Read the speech bubbles, caption boxes and any sound effects from left to right, too. Together with the images, these will tell you the story.

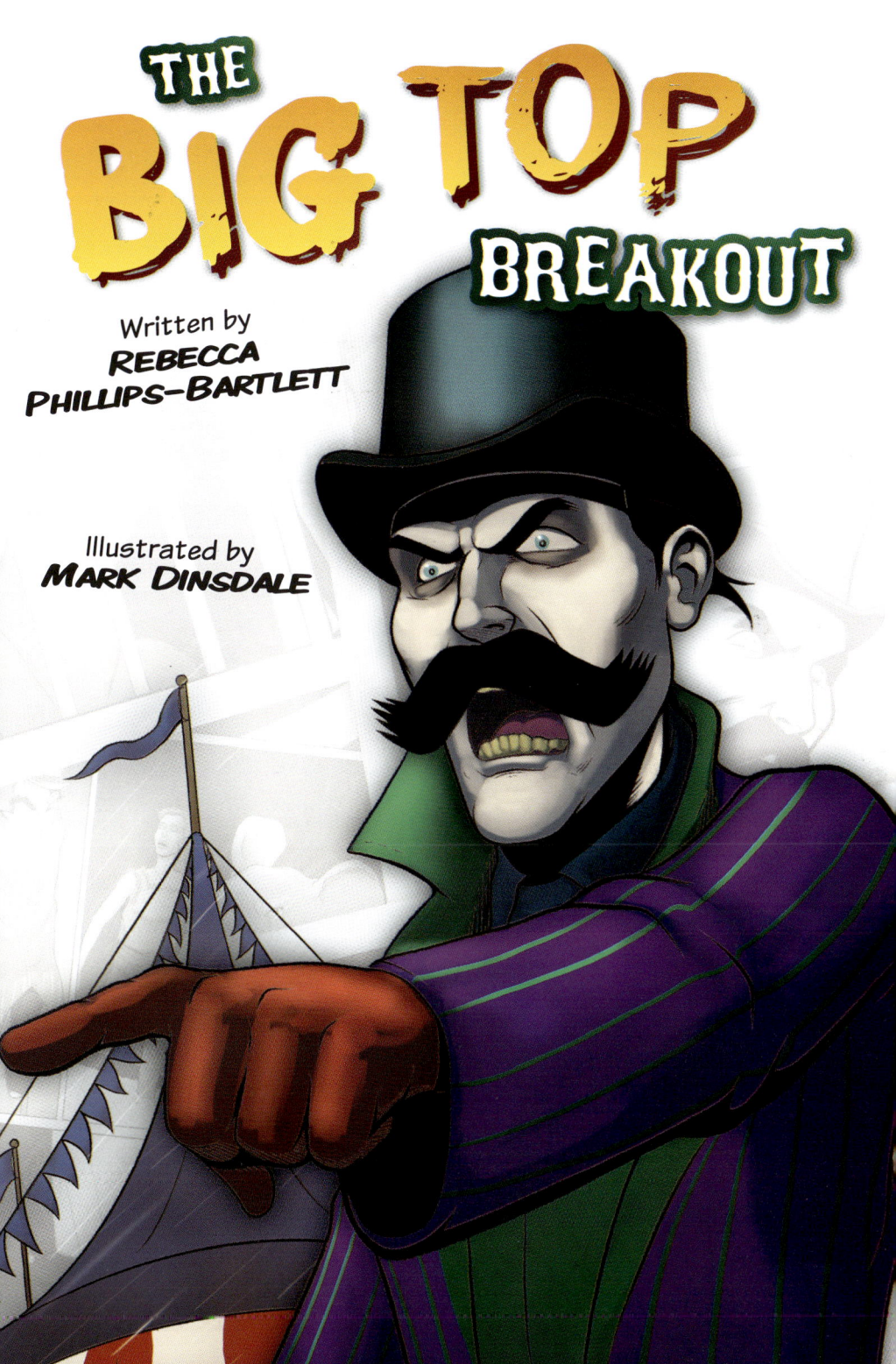

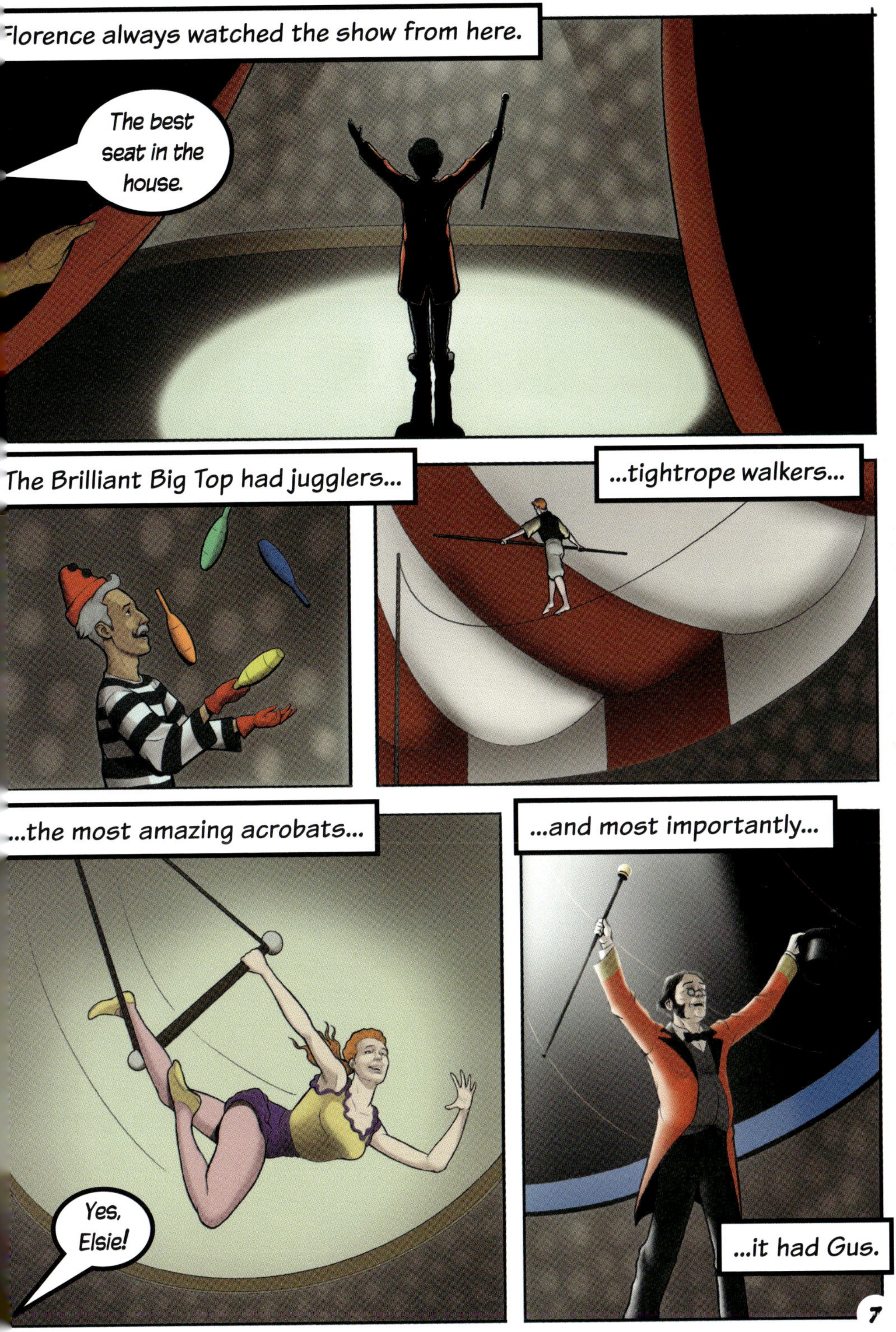

Florence always watched the show from here.

The best seat in the house.

The Brilliant Big Top had jugglers...

...tightrope walkers...

...the most amazing acrobats...

Yes, Elsie!

...and most importantly...

...it had Gus.

> Ladies and gentlemen, this evening was my final performance with you all. I will be handing over my hat and Edgar will...

> I can take it from here, thank *you*.

Suddenly, the circus was filled with the roars and whimpers of strange but amazing animals.

In the week that followed, acrobats managed monkeys...

...jugglers became seal trainers...

...and clowns became animal tamers.

But nothing was going according to plan.

Except for one pair. Florence and Connie were performing fantastic feats almost instantly.

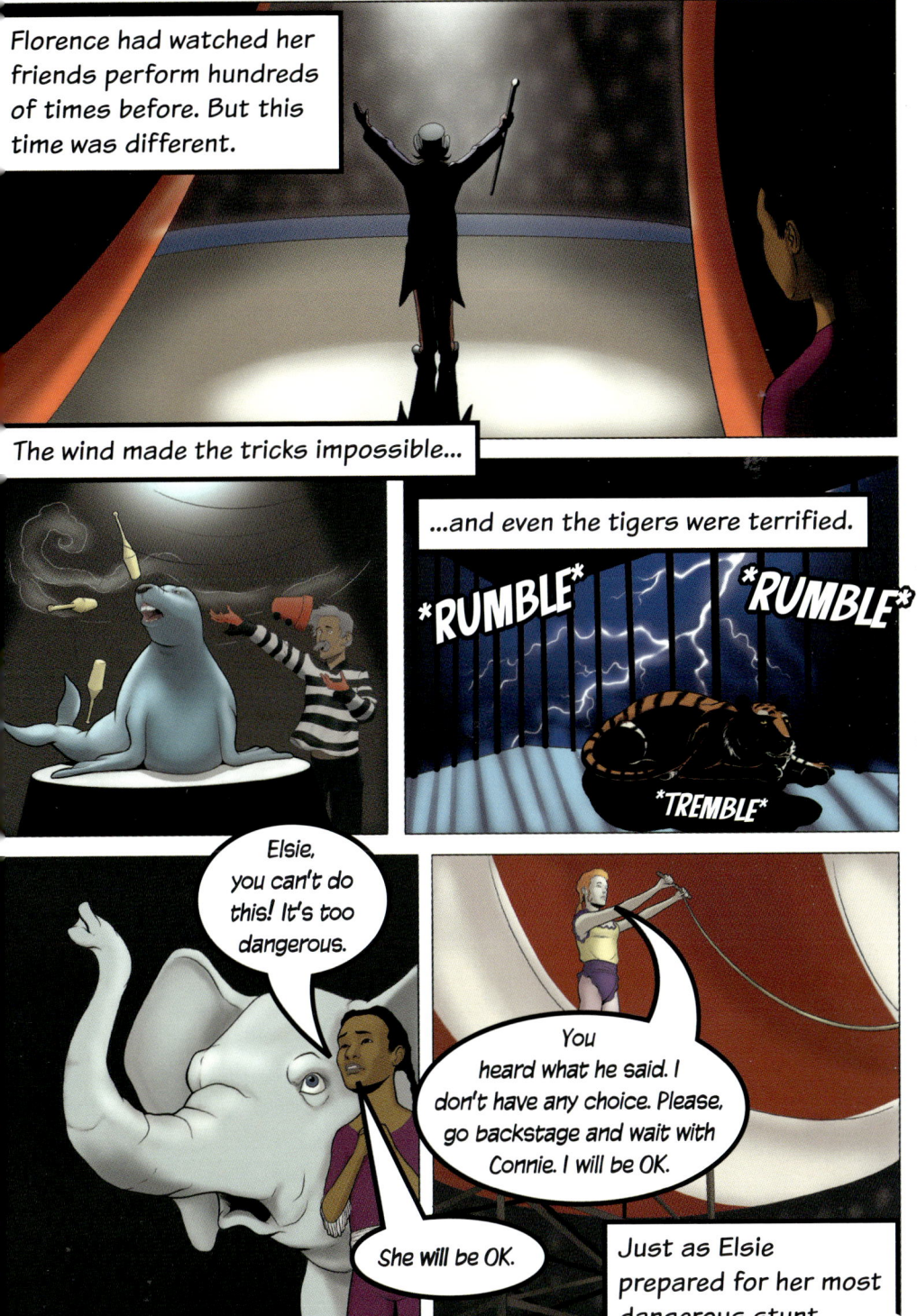

@2024 BookLife Publishing Ltd.
King's Lynn, Norfolk, PE30 4LS, UK

ISBN 978-1-80505-287-6

All rights reserved. Printed in India.
A catalogue record for this book is
available from the British Library.

The Big Top Breakout
Written by Rebecca Phillips-Bartlett
Illustrated by Mark Dinsdale

ABOUT BOOKLIFE GRAPHIC READERS

BookLife Graphic Readers are designed to encourage reluctant readers to take the next step in their reading adventure. These books are a perfect accompaniment to the BookLife Readers phonics scheme and are designed to be read by children who have a good grasp on reading but are reluctant to pick up a full-prose book. Graphic Readers combine graphic and prose storytelling in a way that aids comprehension and presents a more accessible reading experience for reluctant readers and lovers of comic books.

ABOUT THE AUTHOR

Rebecca loves storytelling. When she is not at work writing stories, she can often be found at the theatre teaching, performing or directing. Rebecca lives with her three cats who love to help her write by walking across the keyboard as she is typing.

ABOUT THE ILLUSTRATOR

Mark Dinsdale got his start in illustration drawing dinosaurs and superheroes in the back of maths books when he should've been learning his times tables and has been a professional since 2017 as lead illustrator for two top-notch companies. When not creating captivating art, you'll find them surrounded by three smelly but adorable cats, a wagging-tailed dog, and sharing life's canvas with a lovely girlfriend. Don't be fooled by his weirdly large forehead, his drawings occasionally make people go "that's nice" and it fills him with joy until he realises he's drawn the feet a bit weird.